# Apache Hive Query Language in 2 Days

# Jump Start Guide

_____

Pak L Kwan

Apache Hive Query Language in 2 Days
Copyright © 2016 by Pak L Kwan

All rights reserved. No part of this book may be reproduced or transmitted in any form or by any means without written permission from the author.

ISBN-13: 978-1541081352
ISBN-10: 1541081358

Printed in the USA by JumpStartIn2Days.com

# Dedication

*Dedicated to my family, my team and my students*

Blank page

# Table of Contents

Introduction.................................................................2

Day One ...................................................................3

Chapter One: What is Apache Hive? ....................................4

Chapter Two: History of Hive ...............................................5

Chapter Three: Apache Hive and Apache Hadoop Ecosystem 7

Chapter Four: Hive CLI and Beeline CLI.............................9

Chapter Five: Hive Data Types...........................................14

Chapter Six: Hive Database and Hive Table .......................16

Chapter Seven: HQL  Queries ...........................................30

Chapter Eight: Hive Data Manipulation Language ............32

Day Two...................................................................40

Chapter Nine: File Formats..................................................41

Chapter Ten: Partitioning.....................................................47

Chapter Eleven: Bucketing ..................................................56

Chapter Twelve: Hive View .................................................59

Chapter Thirteen: More SELECT .......................................61

Chapter Fourteen: INNER JOIN..........................................65

Chapter Fifteen: Basic aggregation – GROUP BY.............71

Chapter Sixteen: Conclusion................................................73

# Introduction

We are living in a very fast-paced era. Technologies come and go. We need to pick up new technologies fast. We also need to know how to apply them to our work fast.

I am an enterprise Architect at day and college professor at night. Years after years, I must pick up new technologies very quick, apply them and teach others. Along with this line, I have started to come up with a process that I can learn any key concepts in 2 Days.

Day 1: History of the technology (key concept) and basic / foundation of the technology (key concept).

Day 2: Selected Advanced Topic and Application of the technology (key concept)

To share my learning experience with my team and my students. I plan to create a series of Quick Start Guide. I will help you to learn a new technology in 2 Days. The general format of the guide.

Day 1: History of the technology and Basic / Foundation of the technology

Day 2: Selected Advanced Topic and Application of the technology

Some of the Guides have been used in classes that I taught in the past years.

# Day One

Day one includes Chapter 1 to Chapter 8. On day one, you will learn what Apache Hive is. You will find out the history of Apache Hive. You also will learn how to use Hive command line interface (Hive CLI) and some common useful hive commands. After the day one, you know how to create hive database, create hive table, load data into a table and a simple query to retrieve data from the table.

# Chapter One: What is Apache Hive?

**Apache Hive** is a data warehouse software built on top of Hadoop for providing data summarization, query, and analysis. Hive gives an SQL-like interface to query data stored in file systems that integrate with Hadoop. Hive provides the necessary SQL abstraction to integrate SQL-like Queries (Hive Query Language, HQL) into the underlying Java API without the need to implement queries in the low-level Java API.

Since most of the data warehousing application work with SQL-based querying language, Hive supports easy portability of SQL-based application to Hadoop. Apache Hive supports analysis of large datasets stored in Hadoop's HDFS and compatible file systems such as Amazon S3 filesystem. While initially developed by Facebook, Now Apache Hive is an open source project run by volunteers at the Apache Software Foundation.

# Chapter Two: History of Hive

https://www.qubole.com/blog/big-data/founders-transformation-hadoop/?utm_source=Quora&utm_medium=Answer&utm_campaign=Gil&utm_content=History-of-Hive

Ashish Thusoo and Joydeep Sen Sarma, who were co-founders of Apache. Here is why they said what they created Hive on Facebook.

**Sen Sarma:** From a personal perspective, I wrote some fairly complex Java Map-Reduce jobs when I first started using Hadoop. It became clear to me very that it would not be possible for us to teach our fast-growing engineering and analyst teams this skill set to be able to exploit Hadoop across the organization. At the same time, we abhorred a setup where a small set of data pros would have to be called upon every time analysis of data in Hadoop were to be required.

We knew that SQL was an interface widely used by engineers (for developing applications) and analysts (for analysis) that would require little training. While SQL is powerful enough to suffice for most analytics requirements, we also loved the programmability of Hadoop and wanted the ability to surface it. Apache Hive was born out of these dual goals — an SQL-based declarative language that also allowed engineers to be able to plug in their own scripts and programs when SQL did not suffice. It was also built to store centralized meta-data about all the (Hadoop-based) data sets in an organization, which was indispensable to creating a data-driven organization.

**Thusoo:** We wanted to bring the power of Hadoop to more and more people, and not just developers. Since SQL was a lingua Franca for all things data and is taught heavily in school and used heavily in the industry, by putting SQL on top of Hadoop we made Hadoop more accessible to data users.

# Chapter Three: Apache Hive and Apache Hadoop Ecosystem

Built on top of Apache Hadoop, Hive provides the following features:

- Tools to enable easy access to data via the SQL-like interface.
- Access to files stored either directly in Apache HDFS or in other data storage systems such as Apache HBase
- Query execution via Apache Tez, Apache Spark, or MapReduce
- Procedural language with HPL-SQL

Hive queries are executed using map-reduce queries. Hive compiler generates map-reduce jobs for most queries. Hive provides standard SQL functionality, including many of the Latest SQL:2003 and SQL:2011 features for the analytics. Hive's SQL can also be extended with user code via user-defined functions (UDFs), user-defined aggregates (UDAFs), and user-defined table functions (UDTFs).

Hive is not designed for online transaction processing (OLTP) workloads. It is best used for traditional data warehousing tasks. Hive is designed to maximize scalability (scale out with more machines added dynamically to the Hadoop cluster), performance, extensibility, fault-tolerance, and loose-coupling with its input formats.

Components of Hive include HCatalog and WebHCat.

- **HCatalog** is a component of Hive. It is a table and the storage management layer for Hadoop that enables users with different data processing tools — including Pig and MapReduce — to more easily read and write data on the grid.

- **WebHCat** provides a service that you can use to run Hadoop MapReduce (or YARN), Pig, Hive jobs or perform Hive metadata operations using an HTTP (REST style) interface.

# Chapter Four: Hive CLI and Beeline CLI

Hive CLI is older Hive Command Line interface. Commands are non-SQL statements such as setting a property or adding a resource. They can be used in HQL scripts or directly in the CLI or Beeline.

To show the hive's help page:

To launch the hive command line interface (CLI)

9

```
root@sandbox:~
login as: root
root@127.0.0.1's password:
Last login: Wed Nov 16 15:50:03 2016 from 10.0.2.2
[root@sandbox ~]# hive

Logging initialized using configuration in file:/etc/hive/2.5.0.0-1245/0/hive-lo
g4j.properties
hive>
```

# References:

| Command | Description |
|---|---|
| ! <command> | Executes a shell command from the Hive shell. |
| <query string> | Executes a Hive query and prints results to standard output. |
| add FILE[S] <filepath> <filepath>*<br><br>add JAR[S] <filepath> <filepath>*<br><br>add ARCHIVE[S] <filepath> <filepath>* | Add one or more files, jars, or archives to the list of resources in the distributed cache. See Hive Resources for more information. |
| add FILE[S] <ivyurl> <ivyurl>*<br><br>add JAR[S] <ivyurl> <ivyurl>*<br><br>add ARCHIVE[S]<ivyurl> <ivyurl>* | As of Hive 1.2.0, adds one or more files, jars or archives for the list of resources in the distributed cache using an Ivy URL of the form ivy: //group: module:     version?     query_string. See Hive Resources for more information. |
| compile `<groovy string>` AS GROOVY NAMED <name> | This allows inline Groovy code to be compiled and be used as a UDF (as of Hive 0.13.0). For a usage example, see Nov. 2013 Hive Contributors Meetup Presentations – Using Dynamic Compilation with Hive. |
| delete FILE[S] <filepath>*<br><br>delete JAR[S] <filepath>*<br><br>delete ARCHIVE[S] <filepath>* | Removes the resource(s) from the distributed cache. |

10

| | |
|---|---|
| delete FILE[S] <ivyurl> <ivyurl>*<br><br>delete JAR[S] <ivyurl> <ivyurl>*<br><br>delete ARCHIVE[S] <ivyurl> <ivyurl>* | As of Hive 1.2.0, removes the resource(s) which were added using the <ivyurl> from the distributed cache. See Hive Resources for more information. |
| dfs <dfs command> | Executes a dfs command from the Hive shell. |
| list FILE[S]<br><br>list JAR[S]<br><br>list ARCHIVE[S] | Lists the resources already added to the distributed cache. See Hive Resources for more information. |
| list FILE[S] <filepath>*<br><br>list JAR[S] <filepath>*<br><br>list ARCHIVE[S] <filepath>* | Checks whether the given resources are already added to the distributed cache or not. See Hive Resources for more information. |
| quit<br><br>exit | Use quit or exit to leave the interactive shell. |
| Reset | Resets the configuration to the default values (as of Hive 0.10: see HIVE-3202). Any configuration parameters that were set using the set command or -hiveconf parameter in hive command line will get reset to default value.Note that this does not apply to configuration parameters that were set in set command using the "hiveconf:" prefix for the key name (for historic reasons). |
| Set | Prints a list of configuration variables that are overridden by the user or Hive. |
| set -v | Prints all Hadoop and Hive configuration variables. |
| set <key>=<value> | Sets the value of a particular configuration variable (key).<br><br>**Note:** If you misspell the variable name, the CLI will not show an error. |
| source FILE <filepath> | Executes a script file inside the CLI. |

11

| Function | Hive |
|---|---|
| Selecting a database | USE database; |
| Listing databases | SHOW DATABASES; |
| Listing tables in a database | SHOW TABLES; |
| Describing the format of a table | DESCRIBE(FORMATTED\|EXTENDED) table; |
| Creating a database | CREATE DATABASE db_name; |
| Dropping a database | DROP DATABASE db_name(CASCADE); |

Examples:

```
hive> describe customers
    > ;
OK
customerid              int
firstname               string
lastname                string
Time taken: 2.256 seconds, Fetched: 3 row(s)
hive>
```

# Chapter Five: Hive Data Types

Hive support some common primitive data types which you can find in relational databases. And Hive has also some Complex data types that you might have seen them in relational databases.

Numeric Types:
- TINYINT (1-byte signed integer, from -128 to 127)
- SMALLINT (2-byte signed integer, from -32,768 to 32,767)
- INT/INTEGER (4-byte signed integer, from -2,147,483,648 to 2,147,483,647)

- BIGINT (8-byte signed integer, from -9,223,372,036,854,775,808 to 9,223,372,036,854,775,807)
- FLOAT (4-byte single precision floating point number)
- DOUBLE (8-byte double precision floating point number)
- DOUBLE PRECISION (alias for DOUBLE)
- DECIMAL

Date/Time Types
- TIMESTAMP
- DATE

String Types
- STRING
- VARCHAR
- CHAR

Misc Types
- BOOLEAN
- BINARY

Complex Types

- arrays: ARRAY<data_type> (Note: negative values and non-constant expressions are allowed as of Hive 0.14.)
- maps: MAP<primitive_type, data_type> (Note: negative values and non-constant expressions are allowed as of Hive 0.14.)
- structs: STRUCT<col_name : data_type [COMMENT col_comment], ...>
- union: UNIONTYPE<data_type, data_type, ...> (Note: Only available starting with Hive 0.7.0.)

# Chapter Six: Hive Database and Hive Table

HQL is the Hive query language. It does not fully conform any ANSI SQL standard.

Hive Database:

The term database in Hive is just a catalog or namespace of tables. It is a good way to avoid table name collisions. For relational database folks, you can think it as a schema in the relational database. In Hive, it is common to use databases to organize tables into logical groups. If the database is not specified, the default database is used.

To create a database, you can use to create database statement.

Show databases are the command to list all databases that running under the HIVE. You can also use LIKE and regular expression with 'show databases' command to filter out the list.

Hive will create a directory for each database. Tables in that database will be stored in subdirectories of the database directory. The exception is that tables in the default database do not have their own directories. Below screen shot shows you the default location of the database, dayone.

You can override this default location for the new directory by providing the LOCATION of the user defined directory

You can add comments to the database with Keyword: comment

The USE command sets a database as your working database. Show tables command lists the tables in the working database. In this example, I list the available databases on the server, I choose 'default' database as working database, and them I list what tables are available on the default database.

You can associate key-value properties to the database by using WITH DBPROPERTIES You can view these key-value properties by using descriptive database extended <databasename>:

Alter Database:

Only DBProperties can be added/edited with the altered database command. There is no way to delete or 'unset' a DBPROPERTIES after it is created. No other metadata associated with the database can be changed after the database is created.

Creating table:

You can use CREATE TABLE statement to create a Hive table. It is very like SQL. The general format of using the CREATE TABLE command is as follows:

```
CREATE [TEMPORARY] [EXTERNAL] TABLE [IF NOT EXISTS]
[db_name.] table_name
    [(col_name data_type [COMMENT col_comment],...)]
    [COMMENT table_comment]
    [PARTITIONED    BY    (col_name    data_type    [COMMENT
col_comment],...)]
    [CLUSTERED BY (col_name, col_name,...)
    [SORTED    BY    (col_name    [ASC|DESC],...)]    INTO    num_buckets
BUCKETS]
    [SKEWED BY (col_name, col_name,...)
    ON ((col_value, col_value,...), (col_value, col_value,...), ...)
    [STORED AS DIRECTORIES]
    [
    [ROW FORMAT row_format]
    [STORED AS file_format]
    |    STORED    BY    'storage.    handler.    class.    name'    [WITH
SERDEPROPERTIES (...)]
    ]
    [LOCATION hdfs_path]
    [TBLPROPERTIES (property_name=property_value,...)]
    [AS select_statement];
```

For a jump start a new subject, you don't have to know all the options. You need to aware that the options are here for you to use.

We are going to implement the follow Data Model on Hive on Day One.

Table 1: **Theatres**

| Name | City | State | Zip | Phone |
|------|------|-------|-----|-------|
| Great Escape 14 | Wilder | KY | 41076 | (859) 442-0000 |
| AMC Newport On The Levee 20 | Newport | KY | 41071 | (888) AMC-4FUN |
| Danbarry Dollar Saver Eastgate | Cincinnati | OH | 45245 | (513) 947-8111 |
| Danbarry Dollar Cinemas Turfway | Florence | KY | 41042 | (859) 647-2828 |
| Esquire Theatre | Cincinnati | OH | 45220 | (513) 281-8750 |
| Showcase Cinema De Lux Florence | Florence | KY | 41042 | (800) 315-4000 |

Table 2: **Movies**

| Title | Rating | Length | ReleaseDate |
|-------|--------|--------|-------------|
| Big Hero 6 | 8.5 | 102 | 7 November 2014 |
| Interstellar | 9.1 | 169 | 7 November 2014 |
| Gone Girl | 8.5 | 149 | 3 October 2014 |

Table 3: **ShownAt**

| TheatreName | MovieTitle |
|---|---|
| Great Escape 14 | Big Hero 6 |
| Great Escape 14 | Interstellar |
| Great Escape 14 | Gone Girl |
| Great Escape 14 | Public Enemies |
| Great Escape 14 | The Departed |

# First, set dayone as the working database:

```
hive> show databases;
OK
dayone
default
foodmart
xademo
Time taken: 6.806 seconds, Fetched: 4 row(s)
hive> use dayone;
OK
Time taken: 0.952 seconds
hive> show tables;
OK
Time taken: 0.457 seconds
hive>
```

# Create the table, theatres

```
hive> CREATE TABLE theatres(
    >    name string,
    >    city string,
    >    state string,
    >    zip string,
    >    phone string);
OK
Time taken: 0.644 seconds
hive>
```

# "describe theatres" will list the table definition.

```
hive> describe theatres;
OK
name                    string
city                    string
state                   string
zip                     string
phone                   string
Time taken: 0.702 seconds, Fetched: 5 row(s)
hive>
```

"show create table theatres" will show the create statement to recreate the table theatres

"describe extended theatres" will show us the extended information about the table.

"describe formatted theatres" will show us the location that store theatres table data. As you can see, the older hdfs://sandbox.hortonworks.com:8020/apps/hive/war ehouse/dayone.db/theatres has been created when the table theatres is created. When data is loaded into the table, you will find data files are stored in this folder. Any files that place in that folder will be the content of the table. You can think of one folder per table. There will be multiple date files per folder. This is a very important concept. You will see more when we discuss table partition.

```
hive> describe formatted theatres;
OK
# col_name              data_type               comment

name                    string
city                    string
state                   string
zip                     string
phone                   string

# Detailed Table Information
Database:               dayone
Owner:                  root
CreateTime:             Tue Nov 22 14:22:25 UTC 2016
LastAccessTime:         UNKNOWN
Protect Mode:           None
Retention:              0
Location:               hdfs://sandbox.hortonworks.com:8020/apps/hive/warehouse/dayone.db/theatr
es
Table Type:             MANAGED_TABLE
Table Parameters:
        COLUMN_STATS_ACCURATE   {\"BASIC_STATS\":\"true\"}
        numFiles                0
        numRows                 0
        rawDataSize             0
        totalSize               0
        transient_lastDdlTime   1479824545

# Storage Information
SerDe Library:          org.apache.hadoop.hive.serde2.lazy.LazySimpleSerDe
InputFormat:            org.apache.hadoop.mapred.TextInputFormat
OutputFormat:           org.apache.hadoop.hive.ql.io.HiveIgnoreKeyTextOutputFormat
Compressed:             No
Num Buckets:            -1
Bucket Columns:         []
Sort Columns:           []
Storage Desc Params:
        serialization.format    1
Time taken: 0.712 seconds, Fetched: 35 row(s)
```

I am going to create the rest of tables, movies, and shownat:

```
hive> create table movies (
    > title STRING,
    > rating double,
    > length double,
    > releasedate date
    > );
OK
Time taken: 0.486 seconds
hive> create table shownat (
    > theatrename STRING,
    > movietitle STRING
    > );
OK
Time taken: 0.552 seconds
hive> show tables ;
OK
movies
shownat
theatres
Time taken: 0.285 seconds, Fetched: 3 row(s)
hive>
```

Now we have created three tables in the database, Dayone now. Use "show tables" will list the list of tables in the working database.

By using the Hadoop command: hdfs dfs -ls hdfs://sandbox.hortonworks.com:8020/apps/hive/warehous e/dayone.db, we can find what folder under the dayone database folder. As you can see, I have created three tables in dayone database. There are three folders, and folder names are matched to table names.

```
[root@sandbox /]# hdfs dfs -ls hdfs://sandbox.hortonworks.com:8020/apps/hive/warehouse/dayone.db
Found 3 items
drwxrwxrwx   - root hdfs          0 2016-11-22 14:28 hdfs://sandbox.hortonworks.com:8020/apps/hive/warehouse/dayone.db/movies
drwxrwxrwx   - root hdfs          0 2016-11-22 14:29 hdfs://sandbox.hortonworks.com:8020/apps/hive/warehouse/dayone.db/shownat
drwxrwxrwx   - root hdfs          0 2016-11-22 14:22 hdfs://sandbox.hortonworks.com:8020/apps/hive/warehouse/dayone.db/theatres
[root@sandbox /]#
```

Next step, we will populate the tables. Hive's default record and field delimiters

| Delimiter | Description |
|---|---|
| \n | For text files, each line is a record, so the line feed character separates records. |
| ^A ("control" A) | Separates all fields (columns). Written using the octal code \001 when explicitly specified in CREATE TABLE statements. |
| ^B | Separate the elements in an ARRAY or STRUCT, or the key-value pairs in a MAP. Written using the octal code \002 when explicitly specified in CREATE TABLE statements. |
| ^C | Separate the key from the corresponding value in MAP key-value pairs. Written using the octal code \003 when explicitly specified in CREATE TABLE statements |

## As you can see, theatres is an empty table now.

```
hive> select * from theatres;
OK
Time taken: 0.889 seconds
hive>
```

First, we see the hdfs://sandbox.hortonworks.com:8020/apps/hive/warehous

e/dayone.db/theatres folder is empty. And select * from theatres return nothing.

I am going to copy theatres1.txt (data file) to hdfs://sandbox.hortonworks.com:8020/apps/hive/warehouse/dayone.db/theatres folder and query the table again. Delimiter by default is ^A (control-A). It cannot be shown with the 'cat' command. I will use 'less' utility to show you.

I am going to move a treatres1.txt file into the treatres folder.

Let's query the theatres table again

That is one way to load data into the Hive table. Just copy the data file to the folder belonged to the table. In our example, I copied the theatres1.txt to hdfs://sandbox.hortonworks.com:8020/apps/hive/wareh ouse/dayone.db/theatres/. And then Hive will read the data file when the user submits the SELECT statement. We will discuss more how to insert/load data to Hive table later. There are two kinds of Hive tables, managed table and external table.

The tables we have created so far are called managed table or called internal table because Hive controls the lifecycle of their data. When we drop a table, Hive deletes its data files also. On the other hand, when we drop an external table, Hive remove its metadata from metadata store. But its data files are untouched. Hive does not have ownership of data of an external table.

We can use: 'create external table' keywords to create an external table. The EXTERNAL keyword and LOCATION clause are required to create an external table.

Create a new folder for a new external table.

```
hive> create external table theatres_ext (
    > name STRING,
    > city STRING,
    > state STRING,
    > zip STRING,
    > phone STRING)
    > LOCATION 'hdfs://sandbox.hortonworks.com:8020/apps/hive/warehouse/dayone.d
b/theatres_external';
OK
Time taken: 0.789 seconds
```

Copy                    theatres1.txt                    file
to hdfs://sandbox.hortonworks.com:8020/apps/hive/wareho
use/dayone.db/theatres_external

Then query the theatres_ext table again, you will find 6
rows there.

```
root@sandbox:~
login as: root
root@127.0.0.1's password:
Last login: Wed Nov 23 01:58:23 2016 from 10.0.2.2
[root@sandbox ~]# hive

Logging initialized using configuration in file:/etc/hive/2.5.0.0-1245/0/hive-lo
g4j.properties
hive> use dayone;
OK
Time taken: 2.752 seconds
hive> select * from theatres_ext;
OK
Great Escape 14 Wilder  KY      41076   (859) 442-0000
AMC Newport On The Levee 20     Newport KY      41071   (888) AMC-4FUN
Danbarry Dollar Saver Eastgate  Cincinnati      OH      45245   (513) 947-8111
Danbarry Dollar Cinemas Turfway Florence        KY      41042   (859) 647-2828
Esquire Theatre Cincinnati      OH      45220   (513) 281-8750
Showcase Cinema De Lux Florence Florence        KY      41076   (800) 315-4000
Time taken: 1.032 seconds, Fetched: 6 row(s)
hive>
```

# Chapter Seven: HQL Queries

If you have used SQL before, you will see how easy to use HQL to queries hive tables. That is the one of the main reasons that Facebook designed Hive in the first place.

The basic pattern is SELECT... FROM

SELECT is the projection operation and FROM identifies data from which table, view or nested query. Using the tables that we used previously, theatres, movies, shownat

| Function | Hive |
|----------|------|
| Retrieving Information (General) | SELECT from_columns FROM table WHERE conditions; |
| Retrieving All Values | select * from theatres; |
| Retrieving Some Values | SELECT * FROM theatres WHERE name = "Danbarry Dollar"; |
| Retrieving With Multiple Criteria | SELECT * FROM shownat WHERE theatrename= "Showcase Cinema De Lux Florence" AND movietitle=" Up"; |
| Retrieving Specific Columns | SELECT theatrename FROM shownat; |
| Retrieving Unique Output | SELECT DISTINCT column_name FROM table; |
| Sorting | SELECT col1, col2 FROM table ORDER BY col2; |

| | |
|---|---|
| Sorting Reverse | SELECT col1, col2 FROM table ORDER BY col2 DESC; |
| Counting Rows | SELECT COUNT(*) FROM table; |
| Grouping With Counting | SELECT theatrename, COUNT(*) FROM shownat GROUP BY theatrename; |
| Maximum Value | SELECT MAX(col_name) AS label FROM table; |
| Selecting from multiple tables (Join same table using alias) | select t.*, s.* from theatres t join shownat s on t.name = s.theatrename; |

# Chapter Eight: Hive Data Manipulation Language

Say, you have to use CREATE TABLE statement to create a new table. It is an empty table. The next step you will need to ADD data to the table. Then you might need to modify data or remove data along the way. That is what DML for. With SQL, we will use 'INSERT' for adding data, 'UPDATE for modifying data, and 'DELETE' for removing data. HQL (Hive Query Language) is a little different.

Adding Data to Hive Table:

Method 1: In the previous chapter, we know that we can copy the data file to a table's subdirectory by using Hadoop command: hdfs dfs -put datafile pathofTableDirectory

Data File, theatres1.txt copy to hdfs://sandbox.hortonworks.com:8020/apps/hive/warehous e/dayone.db/theatres directory. It is the time to talk about a concept called Schema on Read. For relational databases, such as MySQL, MS SQL, and Oracle, the database enforces the schema as the data is written to the database from loading utility, from the update, from insert statement. We call it *Schema on Write*. The database has the total controlled which you can look the database is acting as a gatekeeper to make sure data is what the schema or table expecting. If data is not compliance with table definition, data will not be stored/written into the database. On the other hands, the Hive is different. Hive use what we call *Schema on Read*. Hive has no control over the storage. There are many ways to create, modify data. Hive only enforce a schema on Read. If the schema does not match the data file, Hive will return NULL for the unmatched.

Method 2: Idea is the same as Method 1. The data file is needed to be moved into a table's subdirectory. Instead of using hadoop dfs -put command, you can use the Hive's LOAD DATA command.

LOAD DATA [LOCAL] INPATH 'filepath' [OVERWRITE] INTO TABLE tablename [PARTITION (partcol1=val1, partcol2=val2...)]

Where:
[LOCAL]: This is an optional clause. If this clause is specified, the preceding command will look for the file in the local filesystem. The command will follow the file path in the local filesystem.

FILEPATH: This is the path where files reside either in the local filesystem or HDFS.

[OVERWRITE]: Is an optional clause. If this clause is specified, the data in the table or partition is deleted and the new data is loaded based on the file path in the statement.

tablename: This is the name of the table.

[PARTITION (partcol1=val1, partcol2=val2...)]: This is an optional clause for partitioned tables. We will discuss more partition on Day two.

As you can see, I use the data file is located at /tmp/theatres1.txt. I use load data local inpath '/tmp/theatres1.txt' into table theatres2; load the theatres1.txt to hive.

You can find the theatres1.txt has copied from /tmp/theatres1.txt                                        to hdfs://sandbox.hortonworks.com:8020/apps/hive/warehouse/dayone.db/theatres2 directory. LOAD DATA command is the same result as use 'hadoop dfs -put' to copy data file from source location to target location.

Method 3: Use INSERT OVERWRITE TABLE statement to truncate and add data to a table

INSERT OVERWRITE TABLE tablename [PARTITION (partcol1=val1, partcol2=val2...) [IF NOT EXISTS]] select select_statement FROM from_statement;

where:

- tablename: This is the name of the table
- OVERWRITE: This is used to overwrite existing data in the table
- [PARTITION (partcol1=val1]: This option is used when data needs to be inserted into a partitioned table
- [IF NOT EXISTS]: This is an optional clause. The Hive command will create a table in the current database if the table does not exist.

In our example, theatres3 has one record, theatres has six records. After I ran INSERT OVERWRITE TABLE, the record, "AMC West Chester" was deleted and then six records from theatres table have been loaded to the table theatres3.

## Method 4: USE INSERT INTO TABLE to append data into a table:

INSERT INTO TABLE tablename [PARTITION (partcol1=val1, partcol2=val2...)]
select select_statement FROM from_statement;

where:

- tablename: This is the name of the table.

- INTO: This is used to insert data into the Hive table. If the data is already present, new data will be appended.

- [PARTITION (partcol1=val1]: This option is used when data needs to be inserted into a partitioned table.

Method 5: Use FROM from_statement and a set of INSERT statement. That is combined method 3 and method 4 together.

FROM from_statement
INSERT OVERWRITE TABLE tablename1 [PARTITION (partcol1=val1, partcol2=val2...) [IF NOT EXISTS]] select select_statement1
[INSERT OVERWRITE TABLE tablename2 [PARTITION... [IF NOT EXISTS]] select select_statement2]
[INSERT INTO TABLE tablename2 [PARTITION...] select select_statement2] ...;

Method 6: Use FROM from_statement and a set of INSERT statement. That is combined method 3 and method 4 together.

FROM from_statementINSERT INTO TABLE tablename1 [PARTITION (partcol1=val1, partcol2=val2...)] select select_statement1[INSERT INTO TABLE tablename2 [PARTITION ...] select select_statement2][INSERT OVERWRITE TABLE tablename2 [PARTITION ... [IF NOT EXISTS]] select select_statement2] ...;

Method 7: Inserting values into a table from SQL.

This is the traditional way of inserting data into a table in any RDBMS.

INSERT INTO TABLE table_name [PARTITION (partcol1[=val1], partcol2[=val2] ...)] VALUES values_row [, values_row ...]

where:
- tablename: This is the name of the table
- values_row: This is the value that is to be inserted into the table

The following example is used to insert into SQL statement to insert a record into the theatres5 table.

37

```
hive> describe theatres5;
OK
name                    string
city                    string
state                   string
zip                     string
phone                   string
Time taken: 0.664 seconds, Fetched: 5 row(s)
hive> select * from theatres5;
OK
Time taken: 0.202 seconds
hive> insert into theatres5 values('AMC', 'West Chester ', 'OH', '4506 9', '(513) 777-1687');
Query ID = root_20161125015714_0111e879-3329-4714-968f-e8211f25d90f
Total jobs = 1
Launching Job 1 out of 1
Tez session was closed. Reopening...
Session re-established.


Status: Running (Executing on YARN cluster with App id application_1480030794921_0005)

--------------------------------------------------------------------------------
        VERTICES      STATUS  TOTAL  COMPLETED  RUNNING  PENDING  FAILED  KILLED
--------------------------------------------------------------------------------
Map 1 ..........      SUCCEEDED    1          1        0        0       0       0
--------------------------------------------------------------------------------
VERTICES: 01/01  [==========================>>] 100%  ELAPSED TIME: 4 71 s
--------------------------------------------------------------------------------
Loading data to table dayone.theatres5
Table dayone.theatres5 stats: [numFiles=1, numRows=1, totalSize=43, rawDataSize=42]
OK
Time taken: 12.5 seconds
hive> select * from theatres5;
OK
AMC     West Chester     OH     4506 9  (513) 777-1687
Time taken: 0.214 seconds, Fetched: 1 row(s)
hive>
```

In Hive, the value for each column must be provided in the INSERT clause, unlike traditional RDBMS where the user can specify values for specific columns. However, if the user does not wish to specify all the columns, he/she can specify NULL

Updating Data:

Updating data in a Hive table is the traditional way of updating data in a table in any RDBMS. Updating data in a table can only be performed if the table supports Atomicity, Consistency, Isolation, Durability (ACID) properties.

UPDATE tablename SET column = value [, column = value...] [WHERE expression]

38

where:

- tablename: This is the name of the table
- values_row: This is the value that is to be inserted into the table.
- WHERE expression: This is an optional clause. Only rows that match the WHERE clause will be updated

# EXPORT:

There might be the case that you want to write the result of a query to a file. That is the output of a query to be saved into a file.

INSERT OVERWRITE [LOCAL] DIRECTORY directory1 [ROW FORMAT row_format] [STORED AS file_format] SELECT select_statment FROM from_statement.

where:
- [LOCAL]: Is an optional clause. If this clause is specified, the preceding command will look for the file in the local filesystem. The command will follow the file path in the local filesystem.
- [ROW FORMAT row_format]: Is an optional clause. With the help of this, we can specify the row format; that is, the delimiters or the fields terminated by any character.
- [STORED AS file_format]: Is an optional clause. With the help of this clause, we can specify the file format in which we want to save the data.
- Select_statment: This is the column in the clause will be inserted into the file.
- from_statment: This part contains the table name along with the filter condition if any.

# Day Two

In Day one, you have learned to create database, tables and load data into the table. In Day two, you are going to learn what date file formats such as textfile, orc, sequencefile. You will understand what partitioning and bucketing are and when you should use partitioning and bucket. You will learn how to write more complex queries. We will spend some time to go over various ways to populate the table. We will go over more complex table join examples.

# Chapter Nine: File Formats

Hive supports textfile, sequencefile, rcfile, orc and parquet file formats.

Textfile: This is the default format for Hive. The downside is that data is not compressed in the textfile. If you use compressed tools to compress the text files, these compressed files are not splittable as a map-reduce process. It will lead to running a single huge map job to process one big file. It affects the performance in a big way.

SequenceFile: This is a binary file for key/value pairs. That fits well with MapReduce and more compact than textfile.

Worth to notice, Textfile and SequenceFile are a row level storage file format. Hive must read a full row even if only one column is being requested. In this sense, it is the same as traditional relational databases, which are row level based. The row level storage file format is not an optimal storage for Hive if you only need some columns of rows for most of your queries.

RCFile: It stands for the Record Columnar file. It is a flat file consisting of the binary of key/value pairs that are like a sequence file. But the RCFile splits data horizontally into row groups. One or several groups are stored in an HDFS file. RCFiles saves the row groups data in a columnar format by saving the first columns across all rows, them the second column across all rows, and so on. This format is splittable and allows Hive read the column's data it needs and eliminates the unnecessary read.

ORC: It stands for Optimized Row Columnar. It is an improved version of RCFile. It has a larger block size, which is 256 MB by default (RCFile has 4MB, SequenceFile has 1 MB). The bigger block size means it provides more throughput and fewer files and reduces overload in the HDFS's namenode. ORC files stores basic statistics, such as MIN, MAX, SUM, and COUNT, in columns as well as a lightweight index that can be used to skip blocks of rows that do not request. The ORC file format is designed to reduce the amount of data read from the disk. It is recommended to use ORC file format because many new performance optimizations in Hive only work with ORC files.

PARQUET:
It is a row columnar file format. It has a similar design to ORC. ORC is only supported Hive and Pig. Parquet has a wider range of support in the Hadoop ecosystem.

Here is the CREATE TABLE STATEMENT. We can use Stored AS option to specify what file format that the table is used to store data.

CREATE [TEMPORARY] [EXTERNAL] TABLE [IF NOT EXISTS] [db_name.] table_name

```
[(col_name data_type [COMMENT col_comment],...)]
[COMMENT table_comment]
[ROW FORMAT row_format]
[STORED AS file_format]
```

We create a table called movies2 with textfile format. fields terminated by '\t'. \t is TAB, lines terminated by '\n'

```
CREATE TABLE `movies2`(
  `title` string,
  `rating` double,
  `length` double,
  `releasedate` date)
ROW FORMAT DELIMITED
  FIELDS TERMINATED BY '\t'
  LINES TERMINATED BY '\n'
STORED AS INPUTFORMAT
  'org.apache.hadoop.mapred.TextInputFormat'
OUTPUTFORMAT
```

The data file, movie2.txt. Tab "\t" is the delimiter. There are two records here.

```
root@sandbox ~]# cd /tmp
root@sandbox tmp]# vi movie2.txt
root@sandbox tmp]# cat movie2.txt
Big Hero 6      8.5     102     2014-11-23
Interstellar    9.1     112     2014-11-07
```

Load data into the movies2 tables.

```
hive> select * from movies2;
OK
Time taken: 1.318 seconds
hive> load data local inpath '/tmp/movie2.txt' overwrite into table movies2;
Loading data to table dayone.movies2
Table dayone.movies2 stats: [numFiles=1, numRows=0, totalSize=64, rawDataSize=0]
OK
Time taken: 5.012 seconds
hive> select * from movies2;
OK
 Big Hero 6      8.5     102.0   2014-11-23
 Interstellar    9.1     112.0   2014-11-07
Time taken: 1.203 seconds, Fetched: 2 row(s)
hive>
```

As you can see, we can load a text file directory to a table with the textfile format. Only one step.

But you need to have two steps in order to load data to the table with other file formats, there are two tables involved.

The first table is the target table with different file format other than textfile. The second table is textfile format table with the same structure of the target table.

Step 1: You need to load the data to a textfile format table first.

Step2: use INSERT OVERWRITE TABLE <target table> select * from <second table - textfile format>;

The target table, movies_orc with ORC format

```
hive> CREATE TABLE movies_orc(
    >    title string,
    >    rating double,
    >    length double,
    >    releasedate date)
    > STORED AS ORC;
OK
Time taken: 0.754 seconds
```

The second table, movies2 with textfile

```
CREATE TABLE `movies2`(
   `title` string,
   `rating` double,
   `length` double,
   `releasedate` date)
ROW FORMAT DELIMITED
   FIELDS TERMINATED BY '\t'
   LINES TERMINATED BY '\n'
STORED AS INPUTFORMAT
   'org.apache.hadoop.mapred.TextInputFormat'
OUTPUTFORMAT
```

step1: Load data file (textfile) into movies2 first

45

Here are the contents of movie2.txt. There are two records.

```
root@sandbox ~]# cd /tmp
root@sandbox tmp]# vi movie2.txt
root@sandbox tmp]# cat movie2.txt
Big Hero 6      8.5     102     2014-11-23
Interstellar    9.1     112     2014-11-07
```

Load Data local command to load data into the table.

```
hive> select * from movies2;
OK
Time taken: 1.318 seconds
hive> load data local inpath '/tmp/movie2.txt' overwrite into table movies2;
Loading data to table dayone.movies2
Table dayone.movies2 stats: [numFiles=1, numRows=0, totalSize=64, rawDataSize=0]
OK
Time taken: 5.012 seconds
hive> select * from movies2;
OK
Big Hero 6      8.5     102.0   2014-11-23
Interstellar    9.1     112.0   2014-11-07
Time taken: 1.203 seconds, Fetched: 2 row(s)
hive>
```

step2: copy data from movies2 table (textfile) to movies_orc (target table in ORC format)

```
hive> select * from movies_orc;
OK
Time taken: 0.576 seconds
hive> insert overwrite table movies_orc select * from movies2;
Query ID = root_20161128035618_4fe7b935-5d72-43c1-ba5d-ace841d30745
Total jobs = 1
Launching Job 1 out of 1
Tez session was closed. Reopening...
Session re-established.


Status: Running (Executing on YARN cluster with App id application_1480304461685
_0002)
--------------------------------------------------------------------------------
        VERTICES      STATUS   TOTAL  COMPLETED  RUNNING  PENDING  FAILED  KILLED
--------------------------------------------------------------------------------
Map 1 .........     SUCCEEDED      1          1        0        0       0       0
--------------------------------------------------------------------------------
VERTICES  01/01  [==========================>>] 100%  ELAPSED TIME: 5.56 s
--------------------------------------------------------------------------------
Loading data to table dayone.movies_orc
Table dayone.movies_orc stats: [numFiles=1, numRows=2, totalSize=605, rawDataSize=336]
OK
Time taken: 13.919 seconds
hive> select * from movies_orc;
OK
Big Hero 6     8.5     102.0    2014-11-23
Interstellar   9.1     112.0    2014-11-07
Time taken: 0.237 seconds, Fetched: 2 row(s)
hive>
```

# Chapter Ten: Partitioning

By default, a simple query in Hive does a full table scan. This will be an affect the performance (slow down) when querying a large size table. It is very common that Hive table is very large. We need to avoid an unnecessary full table scan. Hive Partition can be used to reduce full table scan. In Hive, each partition corresponds to a predefined partition column(s) and stores it as a subdirectory in the table's directory in HDFS. When the table gets queried, only the required partitions (directory_ of data in the table are queried, so full table scan is avoided.

Partitioned tables in Hive have one or more partition keys based on which the data is broken into logical chunks and stored in separate directories. Each partition key adds a level of directory structure to the table storage. In Hive, the partition key is not necessarily part table definitions. That is the major difference from most relational databases in the marketplace. That look at this example.

We have a Sales table in Daytwo Hive database.

Create table  Daytwo.Sales (
Item_id  string,
Item_name string,
Item_description string,
Unit_price double,

48

Quantity double,
region  String
);


Select * from Sales;    Hive will do Full table Scan.
But how about 'SELECT * from Sales where
region='South';' ?   Hive will also do the full table scan.
There is no the concept of the index in Hive as Traditional
relational database does.  So, we cannot able to reduce the
full table scan with Hive.   It will cost performance if the
table is very large.      In Hive, we can use partitioning to
avoid an unnecessary full table scan. I create another table,
Salea_P with the region as the partition key. I remove the
region column from the table structure.


```
Create table  Daytwo.Sales_P (
Item_id  string,
Item_name string,
Item_description string,
Unit_price double,
Quantity double
)
Partitioned By (region String);
```

In our example, the partitioned key,  region is not part
of the Sales table structure.  We call it virtual column.
When we query the partitioned table, the value of the

partition shows up as the value for the column for all rows in that partition. For example, Select * from sales returns the values for the region column, although the region data is not part of the data file.

When you do 'SELECT * from Sales_P;', A full table scan is still needed. But 'SELECT * from Sales_P where region='South';', Hive does not need to do the full table scan/all data files scan. Hive only need to go to read data files under a south subdirectory.

This diagram is good visual presentation among database, table and partition.

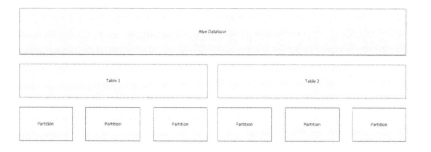

Set daytwo as working database:

```
hive> use daytwo;
OK
Time taken: 0.418 seconds
hive> describe database daytwo;
OK
daytwo          hdfs://sandbox.hortonworks.com:8020/apps/hive/warehouse/daytwo.db      root    USER
Time taken: 0.41 seconds, Fetched: 1 row(s)
hive>
```

Daytwo is a brand-new database, there is no table, so the database directory is empty.

Create Sales table without partition

```
hive> create table Daytwo.Sales (
    > Item_id  string,
    > Item_name string,
    > Item_description string,
    > Unit_price double,
    > Quantity double,
    > region  String
    > );
OK
Time taken: 0.845 seconds
```

After the Sales table has created. hdfs://sandbox.hortonworks.com:8020/apps/hive/warehouse/daytwo.db/sales has also created by Hive.

```
[root@sandbox ~]# hdfs dfs -ls hdfs://sandbox.hortonworks.com:8020/apps/hive/warehouse/daytwo.db
Found 1 items
drwxrwxrwx   - root hdfs          0 2016-12-01 19:38 hdfs://sandbox.hortonworks.com:8020/apps/hive/warehouse/daytwo.db/sales
[root@sandbox ~]#
```

Create sales_p table which it is a partitioned table

```
hive> Create table  Daytwo.Sales_P (
    > Item_id  string,
    > Item_name string,
    > Item_description string,
    > Unit_price double,
    > Quantity double
    > )
    > Partitioned By (region String);
OK
```

After Sales_P has been created, ../../sales_P has created by Hive

```
[root@sandbox ~]# hdfs dfs -ls hdfs://sandbox.hortonworks.com:8020/apps/hive/warehouse/daytwo.db
Found 2 items
drwxrwxrwx   - root hdfs          0 2016-12-01 19:38 hdfs://sandbox.hortonworks.com:8020/apps/hive/warehouse/daytwo.db/sales
drwxrwxrwx   - root hdfs          0 2016-12-01 19:42 hdfs://sandbox.hortonworks.com:8020/apps/hive/warehouse/daytwo.db/sales_p
[root@sandbox ~]#
```

And this directory is empty because I have added any data to the tables now

```
[root@sandbox ~]# hdfs dfs -ls hdfs://sandbox.hortonworks.com:8020/apps/hive/warehouse/daytwo.db/sales
[root@sandbox ~]# hdfs dfs -ls hdfs://sandbox.hortonworks.com:8020/apps/hive/warehouse/daytwo.db/sales_p
[root@sandbox ~]#
```

INSERT data in the Sales table by running these SQL at Hive CLI:

Insert into sales values ('item1', 'Item 1 name', 'This is item 1', 102, 40,'south');

insert into Sales values('item2', 'Item 2 name', 'This is item 2' ,102, 40, 'east');

insert into Sales values('item3', 'Item 3 name', 'This is item 3', 102, 40, 'west');

insert into Sales values('item4', 'Item 4 name', 'This is item 4', 102, 40, 'north');

```
hive> insert into sales values('item1', 'Item 1 name', 'This is item 1', 102, 40,'south');
Query ID = root_20161201200549_42b263d8-a898-4244-bec6-dec1cacfaafb
Total jobs = 1
Launching Job 1 out of 1
Tez session was closed. Reopening...
Session re-established.


Status: Running (Executing on YARN cluster with App id application_1480617294186_0003)

--------------------------------------------------------------------------------------
        VERTICES      STATUS  TOTAL  COMPLETED  RUNNING  PENDING  FAILED  KILLED
--------------------------------------------------------------------------------------
Map 1 .........    SUCCEEDED     1        1         0        0        0       0
--------------------------------------------------------------------------------------
VERTICES: 01/01  [==========================>>] 100%  ELAPSED TIME  5.56 s
--------------------------------------------------------------------------------------
Loading data to table daytwo.sales
Table daytwo.sales stats: [numFiles=1, numRows=1, totalSize=50, rawDataSize=49]
OK
```

```
hive> select * from sales;
OK
item1   Item 1 name     This is item 1  102.0   40.0    south
item2   Item 2 name     This is item 2  102.0   40.0    east
item3   Item 3 name     This is item 3  102.0   40.0    west
item4   Item 4 name     This is item 4  102.0   40.0    north
Time taken: 0.203 seconds, Fetched: 4 row(s)
```

Because I ran Four SQLs insert into statement. Four
data files are created under ../../sales directory. Each file
has only one record.

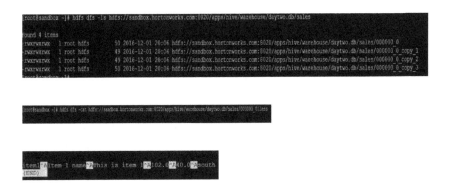

53

As I mentioned at Dayone, the Hive default delimiter is ^A, that you see ^A between column on this datafile.

Let's insert data to Sales_P, the partitioned table

After one record is added to partition = 'south' , you will find one new directory has created under hdfs://sandbox.hortonworks.com:8020/apps/hive/war ehouse/daytwo.db/sales_p

Let's look at the content of the data file: hdfs://sandbox.hortonworks.com:8020/apps/hive/ware house/daytwo.db/sales_p/region=south/000000_0

And it shows the record, "item1Item 1 nameThis is item 1102.040.0". The region column is not part of the data file.

But if I do query the table sales_p in Hive, you will see the region column. That is what we call virtual column. (the partition key is the virtual column)

Let's insert a few more records with different partition key values.

insert into sales_p partition (region='east')values('item2', 'Item 2 name', 'This is item 2' ,102, 40);

insert into sales_p partition (region='west') values('item3', 'Item 3 name', 'This is item 3', 102, 40);

insert into sales_p partition (region='north') values('item4', 'Item 4 name', 'This is item 4', 102, 40);

55

If you list the directory of the sales_p table, you will find there are four subdirectories. Once for each partition values

With Partitioned table, select * from sales_p; hive will do the full table scan. It means hive will read all of the subdirectories and files under the.. /sales_p directory.

select * from sales_p where region='west'; hive will read all of the files under hdfs://sandbox.hortonworks.com:8020/apps/hive/war ehouse/daytwo.db/sales_p/region=west ONLY. That is reason partition can improve the performance.

But, for the " SELECT * from sales_p where itemid='item1';", Hive will do the full table scan because itemid is NOT part of partition keys so full table scan is still needed. It is very important you understand the user query pattern and data to decide which columns should be included in partition key.

# Chapter Eleven: Bucketing

Bucketing in Hive is another way to cut data into smaller segments. This is another approach to improving hive performance by avoiding hive to do full table scan. Partitioning is a good approach if the partition key does not lead to large number of very small partitions. If you have many different values in a partition key and not many rows for each value of partition key. Partitioning may not be the best choice because it will lead to large number of very small partitions. As we know HDFS is beneficial when we have a smaller set of large files instead of a larger set of smaller files. When hive creates a partition of a table, it must maintain the extra metadata to redirect the query as per partition. If we get too many partitions in a table, it would get difficult for hive to manage. Performance will have negative impact. Buckets distribute the data load into user defined set of clusters by calculating the hashcode of key mentioned in the query.

This diagram show us the relationship among database, table partition, and bucket. You can use partition, bucket alone or combine partition and bucket.

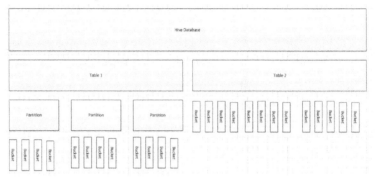

For example, a website wants to do analytics their user click habit. They create a table to track the URL.

Create table url_click (
userid   int,
url string,
sessionid int
)
clustered by (userid)  into 60;

In this case, hive will create 60 buckets.  And the userid will hash into 60 values.  SELECT * FROM url_click where userid = 1234;   Hive will calculate the hash number of the userid, and then only read one bucket instead of doing a full table scan.

We can also combine Partitioning and Bucketing together. For example,

```
create table url_click (
userid   int,
url string,
sessionid int
)
partitioned by (ClickDate string)
clustered by (userid)  into 60;
```

In this case, the data set will be partitioned by ClickDate and then each partition has 60 buckets.

# Chapter Twelve: Hive View

In Hive, the idea of view is like the traditional relational database which is a logical data structure that can use to simplify other users' queries by hiding complex joins, subqueries. Very important to remember!! Once the Hive view is created, its structure is frozen. The change to the underlying tables will not be reflected in the view's structure.

If the underlying table is dropped or changed, query the view will cause an error.

```
CREATE VIEW [IF NOT EXISTS] [db_name.] view_name [(column_name
[COMMENT column_comment],...)]
    [COMMENT view_comment]
    [TBLPROPERTIES (property_name = property_value,...)]
    AS SELECT...;
```

It is like regular SQL to create hive view.

You use CREATE VIEW view_name (columns ...) as SELECT * from anothertable; If you have needs to filter data, you can add WHERE on the select statement.

Here is an example, the sales_view is subset set of data from sales table. The view only shows the item_id and item_description columns from sales table.

```
hive> create view sales_view (item_id, item_desc)
    > as select item_id, item_description from sales;
OK
Time taken: 4.45 seconds
hive> select * from  sales_view;
OK
item1    This is item 1
item2    This is item 2
item3    This is item 3
item4    This is item 4
Time taken: 0.451 seconds, Fetched: 4 row(s)
```

# Chapter Thirteen: More SELECT

In Dayone, you have learned to write simple select statement such as:

select * from sales;
select * from sales where item_id = 'item1";

Daytwo, we will continue to learn more advanced SELECT. Multiple SELECT statements can work together to form a complex query. Common techniques are a a nest, subqueries, join, union.

1) A SELECT Statement acting as a table after FROM:

select item_id  FROM
  ( select * from sales where item_id = 'item1' )  A;

Here Select * from sales where item_id='item1' is called subquery. It is considered as A table which is selected by the first SELECT.

```
hive> select item_id from (
    > select * from sales where item_id='item1'
    > ) A;
OK
item1
Time taken: 0.552 seconds, Fetched: 1 row(s)
```

2) subquery is created by "With" keyword:

In this case, with A as (select * from sales) is the subquery which is used by the second SELECT.

```
hive> with A as (
   > select * from sales)
   > SELECT item_id, item_name from A;
OK
item1    Item 1 name
item2    Item 2 name
item3    Item 3 name
item4    Item 4 name
Time taken: 1.29 seconds, Fetched: 4 row(s)
```

3) A subquery can be also used as part of Where clause with IN, NOT IN, EXIST, or NOT EXIST. We used similar syntax at regular SQL

SELECT * from Sales S
where  a.item_id  IN
(
Select item_id from sales_p
);

This HQL returns any record at sales table that item_id is matched item_id in the sales_p table.

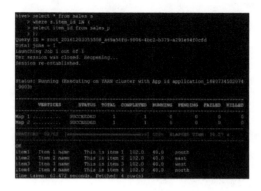

SELECT * from sales S
where EXISTS
(SELECT * from Sales_p p
 where S.item_id = p.item_id
);


The IN and NOT IN only support one column

```
hive> select * from sales s
    > where exists
    > (select * from sales_p p
    > where s.item_id = p.item_id
    > );
Query ID = root_20161203055938_40384a91-4d86-4894-9c64-cebe70ff6c98
Total jobs = 1
Launching Job 1 out of 1


Status: Running (Executing on YARN cluster with App id application_1480734502074_00
3)

--------------------------------------------------------------------------------
        VERTICES      STATUS   TOTAL  COMPLETED  RUNNING  PENDING  FAILED  KILLED
--------------------------------------------------------------------------------
Map 1 ..........   SUCCEEDED      1        1         0        0       0       0
Map 2 ..........   SUCCEEDED      1        1         0        0       0       0
--------------------------------------------------------------------------------
VERTICES  02/02  [==========================>>] 100%  ELAPSED TIME: 7.07 s
--------------------------------------------------------------------------------
OK
item1    Item 1 name    This is item 1  102.0   40.0    south
item2    Item 2 name    This is item 2  102.0   40.0    east
item3    Item 3 name    This is item 3  102.0   40.0    west
item4    Item 4 name    This is item 4  102.0   40.0    north
Time taken: 8.294 seconds, Fetched: 4 row(s)
```

# Chapter Fourteen: INNER JOIN

In this version of HIVE , only equal-join is supported. It is because unequal join is very difficult to implement to MapReduce Job.

In Dayone, we have created three tables:  theatres, movies, and shownat.

```
hive> use dayone;
OK
Time taken: 0.284 seconds
hive> describe theatres;
OK
name                    string
city                    string
state                   string
zip                     string
phone                   string
Time taken: 0.67 seconds, Fetched: 5 row(s)
hive> describe movies;
OK
title                   string
rating                  double
length                  double
releasedate             date
Time taken: 0.585 seconds, Fetched: 4 row(s)
hive> describe shownat;
OK
theatrename             string
movietitle              string
Time taken: 0.62 seconds, Fetched: 2 row(s)
```

This is a very simple relational data model:
theatres.name is matched to showat.theatrenam
movies.title is matched to shownat.movietitle
We can use showna table to relate theatres table and movies table.  It shows which theatres shows what movies.

select  theatres.name,  movies.title  from shownat inner join theatres on shownat.theatrename = theatres.name inner join movies on shownat.movietitle = movies.title;

```
hive> select theatres.name, movies.title from shownat
    > inner join theatres on shownat.theatrename = theatres.name
    > inner join movies on shownat.movietitle = movies.title;
Query ID = root_20161203062721_e2aae552-6342-488d-8b61-e5853db3c2ca
Total jobs = 1
Launching Job 1 out of 1


Status: Running (Executing on YARN cluster with App id application_1480734502074_0004)

----------------------------------------------------------------------------------------
        VERTICES      STATUS    TOTAL  COMPLETED  RUNNING  PENDING  FAILED  KILLED
----------------------------------------------------------------------------------------
Map 1 ..........    SUCCEEDED      1         1         0        0       0       0
Map 2 ..........    SUCCEEDED      1         1         0        0       0       0
Map 3 ..........    SUCCEEDED      1         1         0        0       0       0
----------------------------------------------------------------------------------------
VERTICES: 03/03  [==========================>>] 100%  ELAPSED TIME: 7.42 s
----------------------------------------------------------------------------------------
OK
```

As you can see, it is quite complex already. There are
there Mapper involved.

The result:

```
Great Escape 14 Big Hero 6
Great Escape 14 Interstellar
AMC Newport On The Levee 20      Away We Go
AMC Newport On The Levee 20      Up
Danbarry Dollar Saver Eastgate   Big Hero 6
Danbarry Dollar Saver Eastgate   Interstellar
Danbarry Dollar Saver Eastgate   Gone Girl
Danbarry Dollar Saver Eastgate   Nightcrawler
Danbarry Dollar Cinemas Turfway Nightcrawler
Danbarry Dollar Cinemas Turfway The Green Mile
Danbarry Dollar Cinemas Turfway District 9
Great Escape 14 Gone Girl
Danbarry Dollar Cinemas Turfway Star Trek
Danbarry Dollar Cinemas Turfway Aliens in the Attic
Danbarry Dollar Cinemas Turfway The Hurt Locker
Esquire Theatre Interstellar
Esquire Theatre Schindlers List
Esquire Theatre Fargo
Esquire Theatre The Pianist
Showcase Cinema De Lux Florence Big Hero 6
Showcase Cinema De Lux Florence Interstellar
Showcase Cinema De Lux Florence Gone Girl
Great Escape 14 Public Enemies
Showcase Cinema De Lux Florence District 9
Showcase Cinema De Lux Florence A Perfect Getaway
Showcase Cinema De Lux Florence Star Trek
Showcase Cinema De Lux Florence Aliens in the Attic
Showcase Cinema De Lux Florence Away We Go
Showcase Cinema De Lux Florence The Hurt Locker
Showcase Cinema De Lux Florence The Dark Knight
Showcase Cinema De Lux Florence Up
AMC Newport On The Levee 20      Big Hero 6
AMC Newport On The Levee 20      Interstellar
AMC Newport On The Levee 20      Gone Girl
AMC Newport On The Levee 20      District 9
AMC Newport On The Levee 20      A Perfect Getaway
Time taken: 9.055 seconds, Fetched: 36 row(s)
```

We can add Where clause to filter data:


select  theatres.name,  movies.title  from shownat
inner   join   theatres   on   shownat.theatrename   =
theatres.name
inner join movies on shownat.movietitle = movies.title
where shownat.theatrename = 'Great Escape 14'


```
hive> select  theatres.name,  movies.title  from shownat
    > inner join theatres on shownat.theatrename = theatres.name
    > inner join movies on shownat.movietitle = movies.title
    > where shownat.theatrename = 'Great Escape 14'
    > ;
Query ID = root_20161203063204_058dfa92-d09d-493e-acd8-abb0f104d044
Total jobs = 1
Launching Job 1 out of 1

Status: Running (Executing on YARN cluster with App id application_1480734502074_0004)

--------------------------------------------------------------------------
        VERTICES        STATUS  TOTAL  COMPLETED  RUNNING  PENDING  FAILED  KILLED
--------------------------------------------------------------------------
Map 1 ..........       SUCCEEDED    1          1        0        0       0       0
Map 2 ..........       SUCCEEDED    1          1        0        0       0       0
Map 3 ..........       SUCCEEDED    1          1        0        0       0       0
--------------------------------------------------------------------------
VERTICES: 03/03 [==========================>>] 100%  ELAPSED TIME: 8.17 s
--------------------------------------------------------------------------
OK
Great Escape 14 Big Hero 6
Great Escape 14 Interstellar
Great Escape 14 Gone Girl
Great Escape 14 Public Enemies
Time taken: 13.605 seconds, Fetched: 4 row(s)
```

We can create a HIVE view to hide the complex join:


CREATE VIEW theatre_show_movie_v(name, title)
AS
select  theatres.name,  movies.title  from shownat
inner   join   theatres   on   shownat.theatrename   =
theatres.name
inner join movies on shownat.movietitle = movies.title;

```
hive> CREATE VIEW theatre_show_movie_v(name, title)
    > AS
    > select  theatres.name,  movies.title  from shownat
    > inner join theatres on shownat.theatrename = theatres.name
    > inner join movies on shownat.movietitle = movies.title;
OK
Time taken: 2.559 seconds
hive> select count(*) from theatre_show_movie_v;
Query ID = root_20161203063730_6cb53c11-7a75-40fe-a48a-5f1e076723b8
Total jobs = 1
Launching Job 1 out of 1

Status: Running (Executing on YARN cluster with App id application_1480734502074_0004)

--------------------------------------------------------------------
        VERTICES      STATUS  TOTAL  COMPLETED  RUNNING  PENDING  FAILED  KILLED
--------------------------------------------------------------------
Map 1 .........     SUCCEEDED    1        1        0        0        0        0
Map 3 .........     SUCCEEDED    1        1        0        0        0        0
Map 4 .........     SUCCEEDED    1        1        0        0        0        0
Reducer 2 .....     SUCCEEDED    1        1        0        0        0        0
--------------------------------------------------------------------
VERTICES: 04/04 [==========================>>] 100%  ELAPSED TIME: 10.47 s
--------------------------------------------------------------------
OK
36
Time taken: 12.621 seconds, Fetched: 1 row(s)
hive>
```

select * from theatre_show_movie where name = 'Great Escape 14';

```
hive> select * from theatre_show_movie_v where name = 'Great Escape 14';
Query ID = root_20161203063932_d1b986f7-6ca0-4287-8b5c-5934b12cd8fc
Total jobs = 1
Launching Job 1 out of 1

Status: Running (Executing on YARN cluster with App id application_1480734502074_0004)

--------------------------------------------------------------------
        VERTICES      STATUS  TOTAL  COMPLETED  RUNNING  PENDING  FAILED  KILLED
--------------------------------------------------------------------
Map 1 .........     SUCCEEDED    1        1        0        0        0        0
Map 2 .........     SUCCEEDED    1        1        0        0        0        0
Map 3 .........     SUCCEEDED    1        1        0        0        0        0
--------------------------------------------------------------------
VERTICES: 03/03 [==========================>>] 100%  ELAPSED TIME: 14.72 s
--------------------------------------------------------------------
OK
Great Escape 14 Big Hero 6
Great Escape 14 Interstellar
Great Escape 14 Gone Girl
Great Escape 14 Public Enemies
Time taken: 16.53 seconds, Fetched: 4 row(s)
```

69

OUTER JOIN

Hive also support outer join as RDBMS.

Table A Left outer join Table B where A.col1 = B.col2;

This returns all rows in the left table (Table A) and matched rows in the right table (Table B). If there is no match in the right table, return null in the right table.

Table A Right outer join Table B where A.col1 = B.col2;

This returns all rows in the right table (Table B) and matched rows in the left table (Table A). If there is no match in the left table, return null in the left table.

Table A FULL outer join Table B where A.col1 = B.col2;

This returns all rows in tables (Table A and Table B). If there is no match in the left or right table, return null.

Table A CROSS join Table B;

This returns all rows combinations in both tables/ It is Cartesian product. It is always not a good idea to create CROSS join. It will create a lot of unnecessary rows.

MAPJOIN (The is more advanced and involve a little mapreduce concept. Skip it if you like and come back later) - should put this session it is a special join in Hive. MAPJOIN means doing the JOIN operation only by Map without the reduce job. MAPJOIN reads all data from the small table to memory and broadcast to all maps. During the map phase, the join operation is performed by comparing each row of data in the big table with small tables against the join conditions. By skipping the reduce job, the JOIN performance is improved.

UNION ALL:

combine resultsets of queries and keep duplicates if any.

SELECT STATEMENT1
UNION ALL
SELECT STATEMENT2;

```
hive> select item_id from sales
    > union all
    > select item_id from sales_p;
Query ID = root_20161203084133_069b97d1-a432-4e67-a4fe-9d54e8c0b55b
Total jobs = 1
Launching Job 1 out of 1

Status: Running (Executing on YARN cluster with App id application_1480734502074_0005)
--------------------------------------------------------------------------
        VERTICES      STATUS   TOTAL  COMPLETED  RUNNING  PENDING  FAILED  KILLED
--------------------------------------------------------------------------
Map 1 ..........   SUCCEEDED      1          1        0        0       0       0
Map 3 ..........   SUCCEEDED      1          1        0        0       0       0
--------------------------------------------------------------------------
VERTICES: 02/02 [==========================>>] 100%  ELAPSED TIME: 7.72 s
--------------------------------------------------------------------------
OK
item1
item2
item3
item4
item2
item4
item1
item3
Time taken: 13.85 seconds, Fetched: 8 row(s)
```

# Chapter Fifteen: Basic aggregation – GROUP BY

Hive have several built-in aggregation functions such as MAX, MIN, AVG, COUNT. If you have experience in SQL, HQL is like SQL. These aggregation functions are used with the GROUP BY clause. If there is no group by clause. Hive will aggregate over the whole table.

aggregate without GROUP BY

```
hive> use dayone;
OK
Time taken: 0.254 seconds
hive> describe movies;
OK
title                    string
rating                   double
length                   double
releasedate              date
Time taken: 0.584 seconds, Fetched: 4 row(s)
hive> select count(*) from movies;
OK
17
Time taken: 0.242 seconds, Fetched: 1 row(s)
```

```
hive> select sum(rating) from movies;
Query ID = root_20161203085213_1ec431e7-dc4d-4e1b-9347-28586b8f863d
Total jobs = 1
Launching Job 1 out of 1


Status: Running (Executing on YARN cluster with App id application_1480734502074_0005)

--------------------------------------------------------------------------------------
        VERTICES      STATUS   TOTAL  COMPLETED  RUNNING  PENDING  FAILED  KILLED
--------------------------------------------------------------------------------------
Map 1 .........     SUCCEEDED      1         1        0        0       0       0
Reducer 2 ......    SUCCEEDED      1         1        0        0       0       0
--------------------------------------------------------------------------------------
VERTICES: 02/02  [==========================>>] 100%  ELAPSED TIME: 6.39 s
--------------------------------------------------------------------------------------
OK
137.9
Time taken: 8.553 seconds, Fetched: 1 row(s)
```

## Aggregate with GROUP BY

```
hive> select name , count(title) from theatre_show_movie_v group by name
    > ;
Query ID = root_20161203090431_95141f5a-e347-414b-bad3-29cf1c1e3bc9
Total jobs = 1
Launching Job 1 out of 1
Tez session was closed. Reopening...
Session re-established.


Status: Running (Executing on YARN cluster with App id application_1480734502074_0006)

--------------------------------------------------------------------------------------
        VERTICES      STATUS   TOTAL  COMPLETED  RUNNING  PENDING  FAILED  KILLED
--------------------------------------------------------------------------------------
Map 1 .........     SUCCEEDED      1         1        0        0       0       0
Map 3 .........     SUCCEEDED      1         1        0        0       0       0
Map 4 .........     SUCCEEDED      1         1        0        0       0       0
Reducer 2 ......    SUCCEEDED      1         1        0        0       0       0
--------------------------------------------------------------------------------------
VERTICES: 04/04  [==========================>>] 100%  ELAPSED TIME: 16.93 s
--------------------------------------------------------------------------------------
OK
AMC Newport On The Levee 20      7
Danbarry Dollar Cinemas Turfway 6
Danbarry Dollar Saver Eastgate  4
Esquire Theatre 4
Great Escape 14 4
Showcase Cinema De Lux Florence 11
Time taken: 64.121 seconds, Fetched: 6 row(s)
```

73

# Chapter Sixteen: Conclusion

After you go through these two days' materials. You know what Apache Hive is. You find out the history of Apache Hive. You know how to use Hive command line interface (Hive CLI) and some common useful hive commands. You know how to create hive database, create hive table, load data into a table and a simple query to retrieve data from the table. You have an overall idea what data file formats, such as textfile, orc, sequencefile, that hive support. You understand what partitioning and bucketing are and when you should use partitioning and bucket. You know how to write more complex queries.

The main goal of the jump start guide series is that: I will help you to pick up a new technology/concept in 2 days. After these 2 days, you should be able to understand and apply the technology. Of course, there is no magic wand, these 2 days' materials only are the key to open the door for you. It does not mean to cover everything about that technology.

www.ingramcontent.com/pod-product-compliance
Lightning Source LLC
Chambersburg PA
CBHW070853070326
40690CB00009B/1827